Miracles & Parables

An illustrated retelling of events and
teachings in the life of Jesus Christ

by Peggy Perry Anderson

*We will not keep them from our children;
we will tell those who come later about the praises of the Lord.
We will tell about his power and the miracles he has done.*
— Psalms 78:4 NCV

This book is dedicated to my grandchildren,
Jacob, Céo, Luke, Leira and Ayzen.
And to anyone who seeks to know what God is like.

The Son is the image of the invisible God . . .
— Colossians 1:15

MIRACLES are powerful acts that defy the laws of nature.

PARABLES are stories that help people understand a spiritual truth.

Miracles & Parables
Narrative text © 2022 Peggy Perry Anderson
Paper mosaic & acrylic illustrations © 2022 Peggy Perry Anderson
Summary: An illustrated retelling of various miracles and parables of Jesus

[1.Bible—children 2. Jesus—miracles 3. Jesus—parables]
I.Anderson, Peggy Perry, illus. II. Title
ISBN 9798377115069

All Scripture quotations, unless otherwise indicated, are taken from the Holy Bible, New International Version®, NIV®. Copyright ©1973, 1978, 1984, 2011 by Biblica, Inc.® Used by permission of Zondervan. All rights reserved worldwide. www.zondervan.com The "NIV" and "New International Version" are trademarks registered in the United States Patent and Trademark Office by Biblica, Inc.®

Scripture indicated as NCV is taken from the New Century Version®.
Copyright ©2005 by Thomas Nelson. Used by permission. All rights reserved.

Table of Contents

Creation — Genesis 1:1-31, 2:1-3 5

Adam and Eve — Genesis 2:7, 21-22, 3:1-24 6

Many Prophets Write about God's Plan 7

The Angel's Visits — Luke 1:26-38, Matthew 1:18-21 8

A Trip to Bethlehem — Luke 2:1-7 9

Angels Visit Shepherds — Luke 2:8-15 10

Shepherds Find Baby Jesus — Luke 2:16-20 11

Baptism of Jesus — Mark 1:9-11 12

Great Catch of Fish — Luke 5:1-11 13

Healing a Blind Man — Mark 10:46-52 14

Light of the World — John 8:12, Matthew 5:14-16 15

Good Samaritan — Luke 10:25-37 16

Parable of the Two Sons — Matthew 21:28-31 17

House on the Rock — Matthew 7:24-27 18

10 Lepers — Luke 17:11-19 19

Storm on the Sea — Mark 4:35-41 20

Demons Cast Out — Luke 8:26-39 21

Crippled Man Healed — Luke 5:17-25 22

Parable of Unforgiving Servant — Matthew 18:21-35 ... 23

Widow's Mites — Luke 21:1-4 24

The Good Shepherd — John 10:14-15 25

Jairus' Daughter — Mark 5:21-23, 35-43 26

Greatest in the Kingdom — Matthew 18:1-4 27

Feeding the 5,000 — John 6:1-15 28

The Bread of Life — John 6:26-40 29

A Walk on the Water — Matthew 14:22-33 30

Parable of the Seeds and Soil — Mark 4:1-20 32

Vine and the Branches — John 15:1-5, Galatians 5:22-23 33

Lazarus — John 11:1-44 34

Triumphant Entry — Matt 21:1-11, John 12:12-19 35

Washing Feet — John 13:1-17 36

The Last Supper — Matthew 26:14-16, 26:20-29 37

Gethsemane — Luke 22:39-46, Mark 14:32-41 38

The Arrest — Matthew 26:47-56 39

The Trial — Mark 14:53-65, John 18:28-19:16 40

The Crucifixion — Matthew 27:45-54 41

The Burial — John 19:38-42 42

Jesus Is Alive — Matthew 28:1-7, Mark 16:1-10, Luke 24:1-8 44

Jesus Is Seen — John 20:11-18, John 21:4-14, Luke 24:36-49 45

The Ascension — Acts 1:6-11, Luke 22:69, Matthew 28:19-20 ... 46

New Heaven & Earth — Revelation 21:1-7, 22:1-5 47

Jesus is King of Kings — Revelation 19:11,16 48

God made everything:

Heaven gleaming with angels,
Universe streaming with stars,
Earth overflowing with life.

Adam and Eve
were the first people God created.

He placed them in a beautiful garden.
There, they lived safely among the animals.
They even walked and talked with God.
He gave them all they needed.

God is the Father, the Son, the Holy Spirit in One.
God made everything.

It was ALL good.

You are the God who performs miracles.
— Psalm 77:14

God gave Adam and Eve one warning,
"NO eating fruit from the Tree of the Knowledge of
Good and Evil. If you do,
you will die."

Everything was good until the angel Satan
tried to take God's place.
HE COULD NEVER BE GOD!
God threw Satan out of heaven.

So Satan tricked Adam and Eve.
Satan lied to Eve and said, "If you eat from *that* tree
you won't die! You will know good and evil just like God!"

She believed Satan, not God.
Adam and Eve ate the fruit. They sinned by disobeying God.
Adam and Eve now knew evil.
They could no longer live with God in the beautiful garden.
One day they would die and be punished for all their sins.
And there was nothing Adam and Eve
could do to change that.

Even though they did not listen, God still loved Adam and Eve.
He already had a plan for change. God would send
Someone to rescue people from the power of evil.

"I know that Messiah . . . is coming."— John 4:25

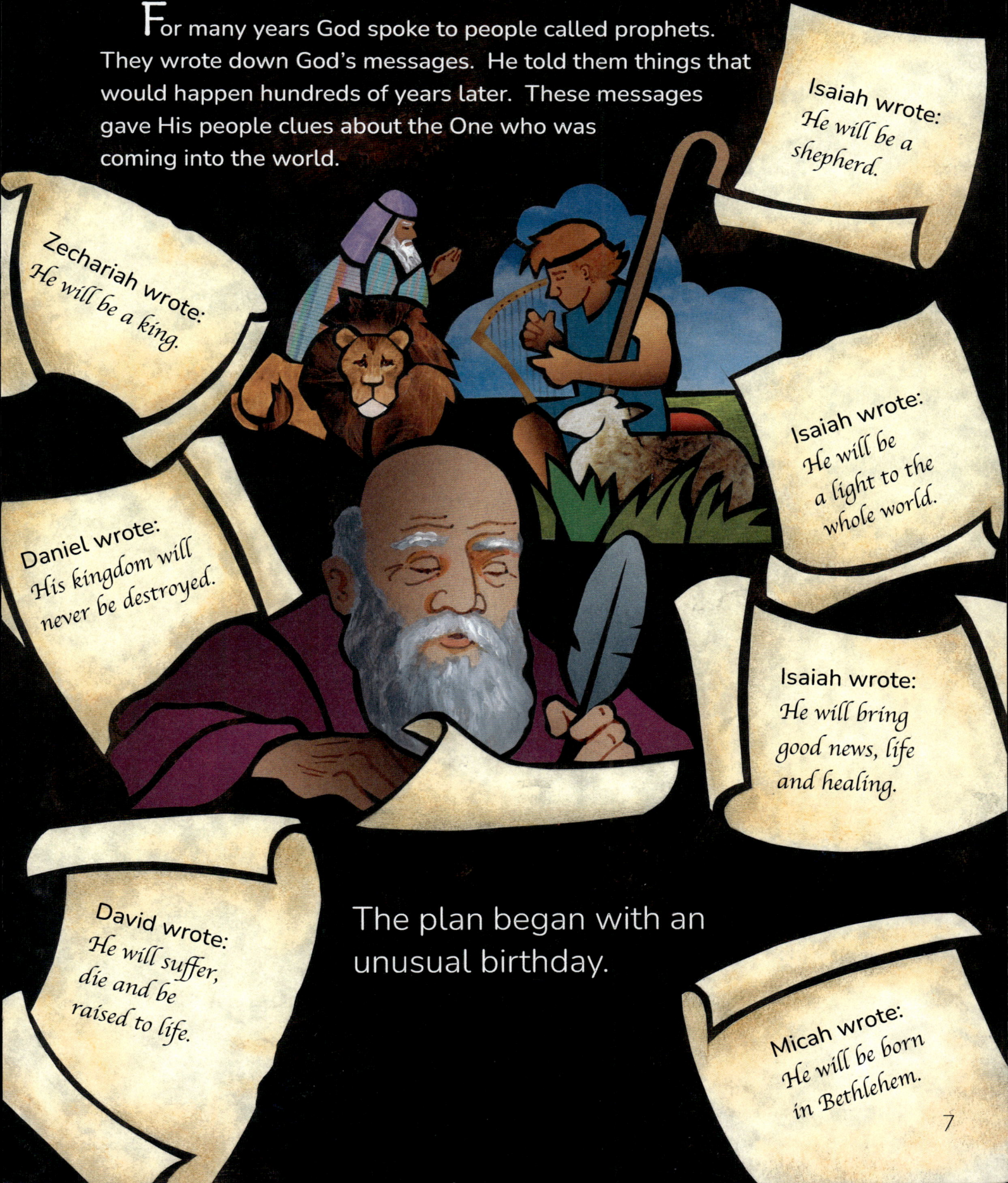

For many years God spoke to people called prophets. They wrote down God's messages. He told them things that would happen hundreds of years later. These messages gave His people clues about the One who was coming into the world.

Isaiah wrote: He will be a shepherd.

Zechariah wrote: He will be a king.

Isaiah wrote: He will be a light to the whole world.

Daniel wrote: His kingdom will never be destroyed.

Isaiah wrote: He will bring good news, life and healing.

David wrote: He will suffer, die and be raised to life.

The plan began with an unusual birthday.

Micah wrote: He will be born in Bethlehem.

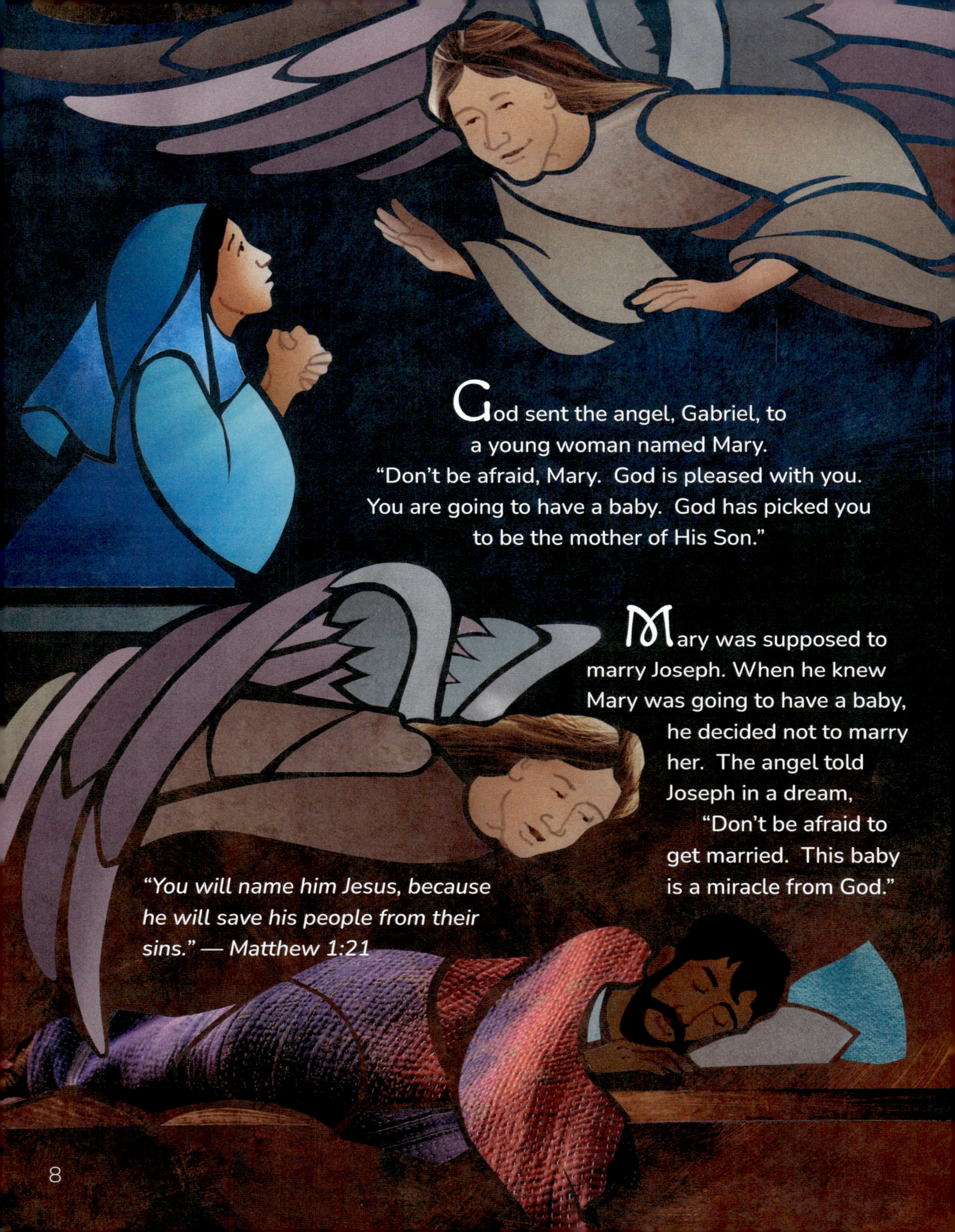

God sent the angel, Gabriel, to a young woman named Mary. "Don't be afraid, Mary. God is pleased with you. You are going to have a baby. God has picked you to be the mother of His Son."

Mary was supposed to marry Joseph. When he knew Mary was going to have a baby, he decided not to marry her. The angel told Joseph in a dream, "Don't be afraid to get married. This baby is a miracle from God."

"You will name him Jesus, because he will save his people from their sins." — Matthew 1:21

Months later, the king ordered everyone to visit the town where they were born. Joseph and Mary traveled the long, tiring trip to Bethlehem.

When they arrived, all the rooms in the inns were filled. Mary was going to have the baby soon! So, Joseph found a stable and made a bed of hay among the animals.

On that dark night, while shepherds watched their sheep . . .

A great light appeared!

An angel announced that a Savior had been born.
"You will find him lying in a manger in Bethlehem," said the angel.
Then the whole sky was filled with angels singing and praising God!
Immediately, the shepherds ran to find the baby King.

*"Today . . . a Savior has been born to you;
He is Messiah, the Lord"* — Luke 2:11

The shepherds found the baby,
just as the angel had said. After their visit,
the shepherds left rejoicing! They told everyone
about the baby Jesus
sent from heaven.

*For to us a child is born, to us a child is given, and
the government will be on his shoulders. And he will be called
Wonderful Counselor, Mighty God,
Everlasting Father, Prince of Peace.* — Isaiah 9:6

Jesus grew up.

It was time for him to teach others about God's Kingdom. When Jesus was baptized in the water, the Holy Spirit came down in the form of a dove. Then God spoke:

"This is my Son, whom I love; with Him I am well pleased."
— Matthew 3:17

One morning Jesus called out to Peter and Andrew,
"Go out to deeper water and let down your net to catch some fish."
Peter and his brother Andrew had fished all night and caught nothing.
They knew there were *no* fish around for miles, but because
Jesus asked, they obeyed. Fish began to fill the net!
The net began to break! Fishermen James and John came to help.

They knew they had seen a miracle!

Those fishermen left their job to do God's work with Jesus.
Jesus called 8 more people to become apostles, too.
Together, they formed a group of 12.

"Come follow me," Jesus said, *"and I will
send you out to fish for people."*
— Matthew 4:19

As Jesus and his apostles traveled from town to town, many people began to learn about him. Crowds began to follow Jesus. "Who is there?" asked a blind man named Bartimaeus. He had heard the crowd passing by. When Bartimaeus found out it was Jesus, he began to shout,

"Jesus, have mercy on me!"

"What do you want me to do for you?" asked Jesus.

"I want to see!" Bartimaeus cried. "Because you believed in me, you are healed," said Jesus. Suddenly, Bartimaeus could SEE! And he started following Jesus.

Praise be to the Lord, for he has heard my cry for mercy. — Psalm 28:6

Jesus taught the people.

"I am the LIGHT of the world.
Whoever follows me will never walk in darkness.
You are the light of the world.
A bright city on a hill cannot be hidden.

People don't cover up lamps!
So don't cover yours. I am the light who
helps you do good.
Doing bad deeds is like stumbling
around in the darkness.

But, doing good deeds
lets others see God working.
Then they thank Him."

"Believe in the LIGHT while you
still have the light so that you will
become children of light."
— John 12:36

Jesus taught the people to love.

"Love God. Love your neighbor. Love your enemy," Jesus said.

A man asked Jesus what he must do to have eternal life.

"What do you think?" asked Jesus.

"Love God most. Then love your neighbor," the man answered.

"You are right," said Jesus.

"But who is my neighbor?" the man asked.

Jesus told this parable:

"A traveler was attacked by robbers. They beat him up! They took everything he had! Then they left him there all alone to die.

"A priest and a religious leader walked by. Neither one helped him. Then a man from a foreign country saw him and stopped. He bandaged the man's wounds. He took him to an inn. He even paid for his care!

"Now," asked Jesus, "who was a neighbor to the injured traveler?"

"Love each other as I have loved you." — John 15:12

Jesus said, "Here is a parable about two sons. Their father told the first son to work in the vineyard. He told his father,

'No! I won't go!'

"Later the son felt sorry. He changed his mind and went to work in the vineyard.

"The second son was told to work, also. He told his father,

'Sure, I'll go.'

"But he did not go. Which son really obeyed?"

Children, obey your parents in the Lord, for this is right. "Honor your father and mother"— which is the first command with a promise — "so that it may go well with you and that you may enjoy long life on the earth." — Ephesians 6:1-3

Jesus taught many people good words to live by. When he finished teaching, he told this parable: "When you hear my words and do them, your life will be like the wise man who built his house on a rock. The strong storm blew and the floodwaters beat on that house **but it did not fall!**

BE PATIENT   SHARE   BE UNSELFISH
LOVE OTHERS   BE THANKFUL
OBEY YOUR PARENTS   BE KIND
BE HONEST   HELP OTHERS
BE A PEACEMAKER   PRAY

"But if you hear my words and do *not* do the things I have told you, your life will be like the foolish man who built his house on sand. The strong storm blew and the floodwaters beat on that house and it fell with a great

CRASH!"

Do what God's teaching says; when you only listen and do nothing, you are fooling yourselves. — James 1:22 NCV

Ten men with leprosy met Jesus. There was no cure for their terrible skin disease. They cried out to Jesus for help. He sent them to show their sores to a priest.

On their way, the ugly sores disappeared! One man quickly returned to thank Jesus for healing him.

Jesus was glad he was thankful. "Were not ten healed? Where are the other nine?" Jesus asked sadly.

I will give thanks to you, Lord, with all my heart; I will tell of all your wonderful deeds.
— Psalm 9:1

One night when Jesus and his apostles started across the lake, a terrible storm began. The wind was wild! Waves were flooding the boat and Jesus was sleeping!

"Jesus! Wake up!"

Jesus woke up. He stood up. He commanded the wind and waves,

"Be quiet! Be still!"

The storm stopped. All was calm. The apostles were terrified!

"Who is this? Even the wind and the waves obey him!" — Mark 4:41

J esus met a man with evil spirits. The man acted like a wild animal.
Not even chains could hold him! Everyone was afraid of him, but not Jesus.

"Get out of that man!" Jesus told the evil spirits.

"Jesus, Son of God, send us into the herd of pigs!" the evil spirits shouted.
"Go!" said Jesus and they did. The pigs went crazy! They ran off a cliff
into the lake and drowned. The man became perfectly normal!
Jesus told him to go home and tell others what the Lord had done for him.

*The Son of God came for this purpose:
to destroy the devil's works.* — I John 3:8

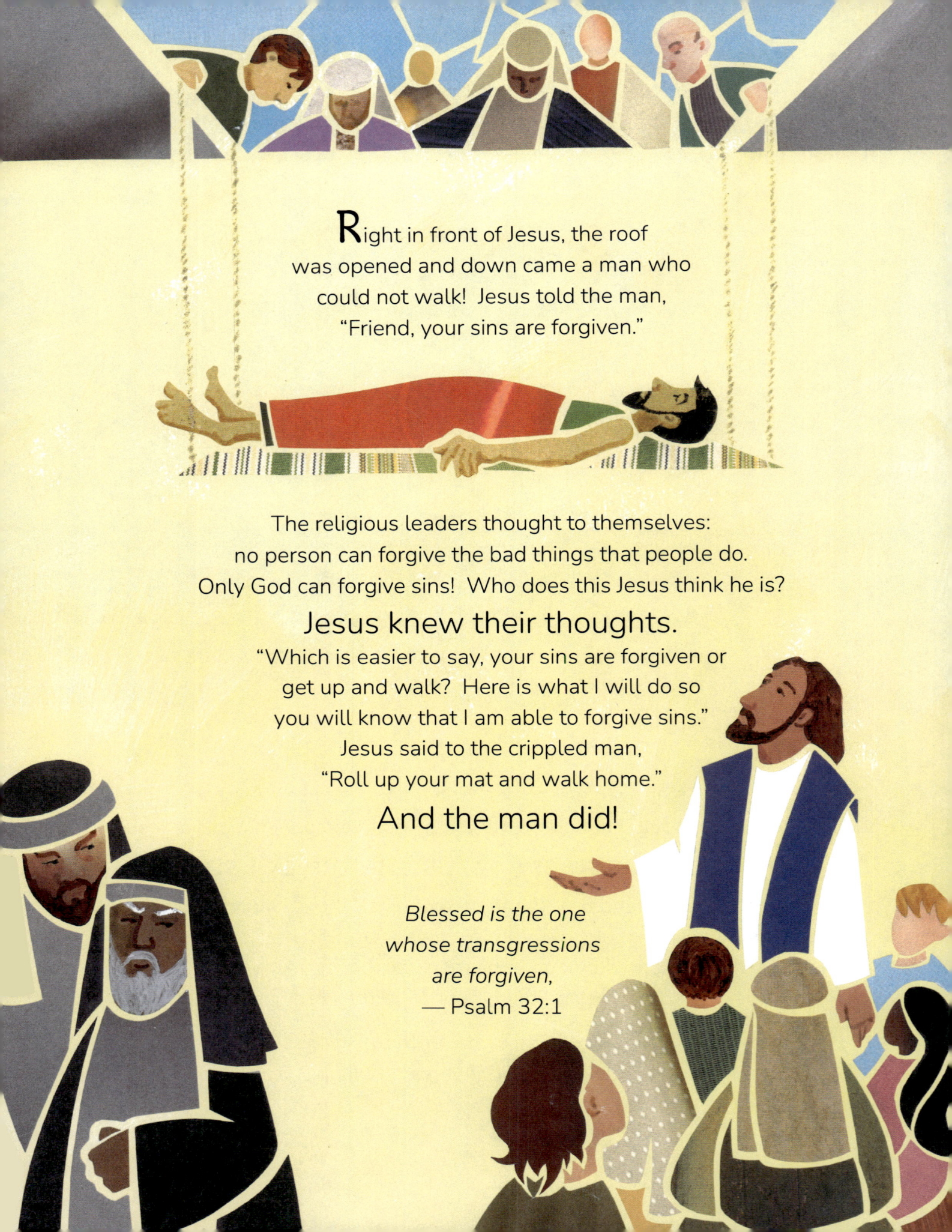

Right in front of Jesus, the roof was opened and down came a man who could not walk! Jesus told the man, "Friend, your sins are forgiven."

The religious leaders thought to themselves: no person can forgive the bad things that people do. Only God can forgive sins! Who does this Jesus think he is?

Jesus knew their thoughts.

"Which is easier to say, your sins are forgiven or get up and walk? Here is what I will do so you will know that I am able to forgive sins." Jesus said to the crippled man, "Roll up your mat and walk home."

And the man did!

Blessed is the one whose transgressions are forgiven,
— Psalm 32:1

A servant owed his king a huge amount of money he could not pay back.

"Please give me more time to pay!" the servant cried.

The king felt sorry for him.

"You do not have to repay me. I forgive you."

Later, the servant found a friend who owed him only a little bit of money. The servant choked him, screamed at him, and had him thrown in jail!

The king found out what the servant had done.

"I forgave you millions! Shouldn't you have forgiven your friend? You won't get out of jail until every penny you owe me is paid back!"

". . . if you hold anything against anyone, forgive them, so that your Father in heaven may forgive you your sins." — Mark 11:25

One day Jesus was at the temple watching people give money to God. A poor, little, old lady dropped two small copper coins into the money box. Jesus asked his followers,

"Who gave the most?"

Then he told them the poor lady had given the most of all. Even though the rich gave a lot they still had plenty of money left for themselves. The poor, little, old lady had given everything she had to live on.

Do you think God took care of her?

"Give, and it will be given to you." — Luke 6:38

Jesus said, "I am the good shepherd."
He told a parable about a man who had 100 sheep.
One of them was missing! He left the 99 in a safe place and went looking for the lost sheep. He didn't give up until he found him. He was so happy to find his one little sheep! He carried it all the way home.

People are like God's sheep. Jesus said he came into the world to find and rescue the lost ones.
The good shepherd always takes care of his sheep.

"I am the good shepherd. The good shepherd lays down his life for the sheep." — John 10:11

Jairus ran up to Jesus.
"Please come heal my daughter! She is about to die!"
On the way, Jairus was told his daughter had already died.
"Don't be afraid. Just believe," Jesus said to Jairus.
Jairus led Jesus into his house. Jesus took hold of the girl's hand and said,

"Little girl, get up!"
And she did!

*Faith means being sure of the things we hope for
and knowing that something is real even if we do not see it.
— Hebrews 11:1 NCV*

Jesus' apostles were arguing about who
was the most important.
"I am the greatest apostle!" said one.
"No, I am!" said another.

Then Jesus lifted a little child in his arms and said,
"Whoever wants to be great in the Kingdom of God must be humble
like this little child. Don't think of yourself as better
than others. Instead, think of their needs before your own.
You want to be great in my Kingdom? Be a servant."

*Humble yourselves before the Lord, and
He will lift you up.* — James 4:10

$\mathcal{M}$any people walked into the wilderness to see Jesus. He taught and healed them all day. It was getting late. Everyone was hungry. All they had was five small loaves of bread and two little fish.

Jesus took the food and gave thanks to God. He broke it into pieces. The apostles handed them out. Jesus fed more than 5,000 people! Everyone was full.

Jesus fed the people food that made
their bodies stronger.
Jesus taught them words of life that
made them kind and wiser.
Then Jesus declared,

"I am the bread of life." — John 6:35

"For the bread of God is he who comes down from heaven and gives life to the world." — John 6:33

After Jesus finished teaching the people, he sent them home. Then Jesus sent his apostles across the sea in a boat while he went into the hills to pray.

During the night, it started storming. The apostles were in danger, but, Jesus saw them. He walked on the water to reach them!

"It's a ghost!" they screamed.

"Don't be afraid! It's me," called Jesus.

When Jesus stepped into the boat, the storm suddenly stopped! This time, the apostles were not terrified. They did not ask each other who this man was. They already knew.

Then those who were in the boat worshiped him saying, "Truly you are the Son of God."
— Matthew 14:33

Jesus taught this parable: In this story, seeds are like God's words. The ground is like people's hearts. Seeds can fall on hard ground, rocky ground, in thorn patches or good dirt.

. . . accept God's teaching that is planted in your hearts, which can save you. — James 1:21

Hard ground:

When the ground is hard, birds eat the seeds.

When people hear with their ears but won't listen with their hearts, the devil takes God's words away.

Rocky ground:

Plants grow tall on rocky ground, but they have tiny roots. The sun burns the leaves and they simply wilt away.

Some people like hearing God's words, but when others bully or tease them about it they simply stop listening.

Thorn patches:

Thorns choke plants. This keeps the plants from growing fruit or flowers.

Worry keeps people who hear God's words from growing fruit of the Spirit in their lives.

Good ground:

Seeds in good dirt grow strong plants. These plants have lots of fruit.

The hearts of people who love God and listen to his words have much fruit of the Spirit. They share God's love with others.

Jesus told his apostles, "I am the vine.
You are the branches. The branches grow the fruit. But they cannot do it without being attached to the vine.

If you love me, obey my words.
Then you will be close to me and can grow lots of fruit."
Fruits are the good things Jesus' followers think, do, say, and feel that help lead others to Jesus and make God glad.

The fruit of the Spirit is love, joy, peace, patience, kindness, goodness, faithfulness, gentleness, self-control. — Galatians 5:22-23

Jesus was far away when he got a message from his friends,
Mary and Martha: Please come and heal our brother, Lazarus. He is very sick!
When Jesus finally arrived, Lazarus had been dead four days!
Mary and Martha were crying. Jesus cried too.
At the cave where Lazarus was buried, Jesus commanded the
stone to be rolled away. Jesus prayed. Then he called, "Lazarus, come out!"
The dead man came out of the cave.

Lazarus was alive!

Jesus told her, "I am the resurrection and the life. The one who believes in me will live, even though they die." — John 11:25

The people who saw Jesus raise Lazarus from the dead went everywhere telling everyone. One day crowds gathered outside the city of Jerusalem. As Jesus rode on a donkey, the people honored him by throwing their coats on the road, waving palm branches, and shouting,

"Hosanna! Blessed is the King of Israel!"

They thought Jesus would become the king of their country. But God had a much greater plan.

"See, your king comes to you, righteous and victorious, lowly and riding on a donkey," — Zechariah 9:9

The religious leaders were jealous.

"Look! The whole world is following him!"

They decided to secretly kill Jesus.

Jesus and his apostles were about to eat the Passover.
This special meal reminded the people of being rescued by God from slavery.
Before they ate, Jesus began to wash the apostles' feet.
This was something only servants did.

"You are not washing my feet!" said Peter.

But Jesus washed them anyway. He even washed the feet of Judas.
Jesus knew Judas was only pretending to be a friend.

"Even though I am your Lord and Teacher," Jesus explained,
"I am still serving you. You should serve each other, too."

"As I have loved you, so you must love one another." — John 13:34

As they ate, Jesus told his apostles that this special meal would have new meaning.

The bread would remind them of his broken body. The wine would remind them of his blood. Tomorrow he would die on a cross so people could be rescued from slavery to sin.

"Look, the Lamb of God, who takes away the sin of the world!"
— John 1:29

Judas left the dinner early. "You can capture Jesus tonight in Gethsemane," he told the religious leaders.

They paid him 30 silver coins.

Jesus and his apostles walked to the garden of Gethsemane. He knew that soon he would be suffering on a cross. He was very, very afraid. While his apostles slept, he prayed to God three times.

"Father, must I do this? But, I will do what you want." An angel came to help Jesus be brave. Then Judas arrived with soldiers.

"My Father . . . may your will be done." — Matthew 26:42

Judas greeted Jesus. The soldiers grabbed him.
Peter swung his sword and cut off the ear of one of Jesus' enemies!
"Stop! No more of this!" cried Jesus. "Don't you know I could ask my Father for thousands of angels to help us?" But, Jesus did not ask for angels.
He knew he must finish his Father's plan.
So, Jesus healed the man's ear.
Then he let the soldiers tie him up and take him away.

"But I say to you, love your enemies. Pray for those who hurt you. If you do this, you will be true children of your Father in heaven." — Matthew 5:44-45 NCV

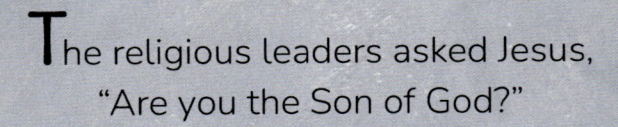

The religious leaders asked Jesus,
"Are you the Son of God?"

"I am," said Jesus.

The religious leaders did not believe him.
They insulted, slapped and spit upon the Son of God.

They took him to the ruler Pilate.
Pilate asked Jesus, "Are you a king?"

"I am," said Jesus,
"but my kingdom is not of this world."

Pilate knew Jesus had done nothing wrong.
Pilate should have let him go.
Instead, Pilate pleased the people.

The soldiers insulted, whipped and spit upon the King of Heaven.
They put a crown of thorns on his head and hit him over and over.
Then they nailed him on a cross to die.

*Jesus said, "Father, forgive them, for they do not know
what they are doing." — Luke 23:34*

Darkness covered the sky as Jesus hung on the cross. The earth shook! The rocks split! Tombs broke open! The soldiers at the cross were terrified! They cried out,

"Surely he was the Son of God!"
— Matthew 27:54

The greatest miracle of love was done. Jesus, the Son of God, chose to suffer the punishment for the sins of all people so anyone can be forgiven!

For God so loved the world that he gave his one and only Son, that whoever believes in him shall not perish but have eternal life.
— John 3:16

All was quiet — day and night.
Then early Sunday morning before the Sun came up . . .

the Earth quaked!

An angel came and rolled the stone away!

Jesus was
ALIVE!

"This is what is written: The Messiah will suffer and rise from the dead on the third day,"
— Luke 24:46

Mary Magdalene saw Jesus.

"Tell my brothers, the apostles, I will soon go up to God, my Father and your Father," he said.

All who believe in Jesus become part of God's family.

Jesus defeated the devil!

The apostles saw Jesus. He filled their net again to remind them to trust in him.

Those who trust Jesus will live with God forever.

Jesus defeated death!

Many followers saw Jesus.

"Peace! There is forgiveness for all who love and obey me," he said.

For those who love Jesus there is *no* punishment.

Jesus defeated sin!

"I am the Living One; I was dead, and now look, I am alive for ever and ever!" — Revelation 1:18

Jesus was going back to heaven.

Jesus instructed his followers to go to all nations and tell everyone what God has done. "Make new followers. Baptize them and teach them my commands."

Jesus was sending the Holy Spirit to live in the hearts of his followers. The Holy Spirit would help them:

Remember the words of Jesus, obey the commands of God, and love one another.

Jesus promised to return again! Then he floated up to heaven. He is on his throne next to God.

Jesus rules over all!

God is the One who raised Christ from the dead, and he will give life through his Spirit that lives in you.
— Romans 8:11 NCV

One day God's children will live in a new heaven and a new earth. It will be full of goodness, joy, health, light and life; because in God's Kingdom there will be no sin, sadness, sickness, darkness, or death ever again.

God has freed us from the power of darkness, and He brought us into the Kingdom of his dear Son. The Son paid for our sins, and in him we have forgiveness.
— Colossians 1:13,14 NCV

Jesus is and forever will be . . .

KING OF KINGS

LORD OF LORDS

Revelation 3:14

The Gospel means Good News

🖤 God created and loves all people. But all people sin.
For all have sinned and fall short of the glory of God. — Romans 3:23

❤️ God is Holy (sinless) and cannot live with sin. But God still loves people.
For God so loved the world that he gave his one and only Son, that whoever believes in him shall not perish but have eternal life.— John 3:16

ALL WHO HEAR THIS GOOD NEWS AND

💔 Feel sad that they have hurt God and others and repent (choose to change),
Godly sorrow brings repentance that leads to salvation — 2 Cor. 7:10

❤️ Believe with all their heart that Jesus died for them,
. . . if you confess with your mouth, "Jesus is Lord," and believe in your heart that God raised him from the dead, you will be saved. - Rom. 10:10

👄

✝️ Are baptized in water to show the death, burial and resurrection of Jesus,
When we were baptized, we were buried with Christ and shared his death. So, just as Christ was raised from the dead by the wonderful power of the Father, we also can live a new life. — Romans 6:4 NCV

THESE ARE FOREVER, NEW, RESCUED, FORGIVEN CHILDREN OF GOD!

Do you believe?

Names of Jesus
and what that means for us

CREATOR/GOD
He designed us

MESSIAH or CHRIST
Our King chosen by God

SON OF MAN
He understands us

JESUS
He saves us from our sins

COUNSELOR
We can talk to him about anything

MIGHTY GOD
He helps us with power

EVERLASTING FATHER
He is a Father to us always

PRINCE OF PEACE
He calms our fears and anger

BELOVED SON OF GOD
He loves us as His Father does

PHYSICIAN
He heals our body, soul, and spirit

LIGHT OF THE WORLD
He shows the lost the way to the Heavenly home

THE ROCK
His words keep our souls safe

RULER OF EARTH
He controls the laws of nature

FULL OF GRACE
He gives forgiveness

GOOD SHEPHERD
He guides and protects us

BREAD OF LIFE
He keeps our souls healthy

THE VINE
He makes us able to be good

THE LIFE
He defeated death for us

SERVANT
He cares for our needs

LAMB OF GOD
He is the sinless sacrifice for us

SUFFERING SAVIOR
Took our punishment to save us from being separated from God

THE LIVING ONE
He lives forever so we can, too

KING OF KINGS
He is Ruler over everything

In the Bible you can read more about Jesus. Matthew, Mark, Luke and John tell about His life.

Made in the USA
Middletown, DE
23 September 2023